THE
BLUFFER'S GUIDE®
TO
RUGBY

ALEXANDER C. RAE

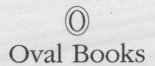

Oval Books

Published by Oval Books
335 Kennington Road
London SE11 4QE
United Kingdom

Telephone: +44 (0)20 7582 7123
Fax: +44 (0)20 7582 1022
E-mail: info@ovalbooks.com
Web site: www.ovalbooks.com

First published by Ravette Books, 1992
Reprinted/updated: 1993,1996,1997,1998

First published by Oval Books, 1999
Reprinted 1999
Revised 2000, 2001

Series Editor – Anne Tauté

Cover designer – Jim Wire, Quantum
Printer – Cox & Wyman Ltd
Producer – Oval Projects Ltd

The Bluffer's Guides® series is based
on an original idea by Peter Wolfe.

The Bluffer's Guide®, The Bluffer's Guides®,
Bluffer's®, and Bluff Your Way® are
Registered Trademarks.

ISBN: 1-902825-96-9

CONTENTS

INTRODUCTION

Many people regard bluffing in the game of rugby as impossible. They reason that it is a highly skilful game which needs exceptional levels of fitness and personal courage. A true bluffer knows better.

Perhaps at international, district, county or even top class club rugby level there is a certain need for these schoolboy hero qualities. But at ground level, things are different.

Here, in many cases, skill could be regarded as a distinct disadvantage and is certain to make you very unpopular with your team mates. Personal courage is needed, but the courage that really counts is being able to go on a drinking spree with people who have made alcohol consumption an art form. This is more damaging to your health than the average game.

Despite the law makers' attempt to make rugby faster and more exciting, it is still the only contact sport where you can get away with the same fitness levels as the average professional darts player. Fitness is like many elements of rugby. It should be talked about a lot but thankfully little attention needs to be paid to it.

The novice may also, mistakenly, believe that he has to look like a 'rugby player' before he can bluff successfully. This shows a basic lack of understanding of the game. This great sport is so diverse and varied that all shapes and sizes are catered for. Fat people, thin people and small people with nervous tics all regularly get a game in one team or other. In the lower teams of some smaller clubs, people in wheelchairs, people with walking sticks and people who can hardly stand up for more than five minutes can often get a game (especially if they are prepared to play on the wing). So no matter what you look like, by using our 'Pick a Position' method any physical inadequacy can be accommodated.

In contrast, people may think that it is easy to bluff in a non-playing capacity. For instance, anyone who has even a smattering of the laws can be readily accepted as an expert. This is due to the fact that most players have only a vague grasp of the regulations and have never found it a handicap in their playing careers. Spectators never know what is happening. They only know that the referee is wrong.

But trying to pass yourself off as an expert by learning the laws is not as easy as it looks. Not only is rugby a wilfully complicated game, as soon as you get the hang of one set of laws the governing bodies change them. The only thing that is predictable about these changes is that they always affect the part of the game you liked the best and generally spoil it. It is traditional to blame them on the Southern hemisphere rugby unions if you live in the Northern hemisphere, and vice versa.

So, rather than trying to learn the laws learn the bluffer's all-purpose 'Suitable Law Interpretations' which can be applied to any referee's decision with impunity. The way many referees interpret the laws, your suggestion is just as likely to be correct as theirs.

But the real bluffer will not be content with merely standing on the side lines. This book will give you not only a few easy-to-learn hints and techniques that will allow you to be accepted as an expert ex-rugby player, but also the key to the ultimate bluff – how to play a whole game (or even several seasons) of club rugby, without anyone noticing that you can't play the game.

THE BASICS

The History

Everyone knows that in 1823 William Webb Ellis, a pupil at Rugby School, invented Rugby Football. Ellis caught the ball while playing football and ran at his opponents with the ball in his hands. Even today most rugby players haven't a clue about the laws of the game they are playing, either.

Early forms of rugby were only vaguely like the present-day game. For instance, at that time there were 20 people in each team. Nowadays a lot of teams are lucky to get 15 on a Saturday and Rugby League teams never seem to be able to get more than 13.

The most important thing to remember is that there is a difference between Rugby Union and Rugby League. To suggest that there are any similarities is regarded, by both sides, as slightly more serious than high treason.

Rugby League came about when, in 1893, several clubs in the North of England hit upon the revolutionary notion that if you were going to get knocked about on a Saturday afternoon you should at least be entitled to recompense for 'loss of time at work'. The vast majority of the rugby clubs recognised this for what it was – an ill-disguised attempt to allow working men to play rugby. Today, a mere 100 years later, the ill-feeling has not really had enough time to settle down and it is important to spit on the floor and cross yourself every time you hear the **'other code'** mentioned.

Rugby League is played in most of the countries where Rugby Union is played (in France they sometimes seem confused as to what code they are playing).

In Britain it is confined to the North of England, where its main function at one time seemed to be to ensure that the Welsh Rugby Union international team was always under strength.

At the higher levels, Rugby League is professional or semi-professional. Because Yorkshire teams were so closely involved with the formation of the sport, the number of players has been reduced to 13 on the grounds that it cuts the wages' bill.

Rugby League is based on the theory that those who support it cannot remember 3,000 laws, so the game has been reduced to one: 'Run until someone tackles you.' As such, there is virtually no opportunity to bluff in the game and hereafter all references are to Rugby Union.

The Myths

The key to ensuring your acceptance in rugby circles is knowing both the myths and the realities of the game. The myths perpetuated by rugby players have evolved to persuade the public that rugby is really as exciting, violent and skilful as it looks at international level. It is important you play your part in their support and development.

The public's perception of rugby, and the game as the average club player knows it, have very little in common. Never appear surprised or shocked by how far the myths differ from reality. To the public, rugby is a sport where 30 big, strong, fit, violent men run round a pitch for 80 minutes knocking hell out of each other. After which, they believe, these 30 men spend the evening drinking prodigious amounts of beer, singing rude songs and playing interminable practical jokes that usually involve policemen's helmets.

In reality, it is not nearly as sophisticated as this.

Myth 1 – You have to be fit to play rugby

While the international game has the same laws as the game that is played at club level, it is as similar to the club game as sumo wrestling is to petit point.

For a start, you don't do anything for a whole 80 minutes in most games of rugby, especially not running around. Forwards spend half the time standing about in lineouts and leaning against each other in scrums. Backs, during these periods, stand about watching the forwards standing about.

Then there is time taken up with kick-offs, penalties, free-kicks, conversions and injuries. With any luck you should be able to reduce the amount of time when you actually could run around to about three and a half minutes.

Some players (particularly props) have been known to play for an entire rugby career without ever getting beyond a brisk walk in any game. Many will openly warn you that it is when players start jogging about the pitch and knocking into each other by mistake that accidents happen.

Myth 2 – Rugby is dangerous

Another significant myth to push is the danger of the game. A member of the public, meeting a rugby player for the first time, will often say something guileless like 'It must be dangerous to play rugby'. The official answer is to insist that rugby has far less injuries than games like hockey or lacrosse or soccer (where points are given to injured players for artistic merit).

You then go on to regale the listener with a list of your past injuries taking particular delight in describing broken bones and suppurating wounds and showing scars (where suitable). Any scar will do. Everything from nettle rash to appendectomy scars have been used as spurious rugby injuries.

Myth 3 – Rugby Union is now professional

The word 'professionalism' will not apply in any way to any club you would want to play for. Not only will you not get paid for playing for the 5th XV, you will actually be expected to spend a small fortune over the club bar for the pleasure of getting knocked about on a Saturday afternoon.

Professionalism actually only affects first teams of about ten clubs who now have to pay tax on their boot money.

Myth 4 – Once you walk off the pitch everything is forgotten

As you stand in front of the mirror tentatively dabbing at the neat set of stud marks across the bridge of your nose, it takes a particular kind of person to say 'Oh well, that's all forgotten about' – the kind of person who is not a rugby player.

In the club-house everything may well be polite. After ten pints, everything may be quite friendly. But when you next see the player who stood on you lying face-up at the bottom of the ruck, memories tend to come flooding back.

There is always one team for every club (usually the side from the nearest town or village) whose every misdemeanour is not only remembered but brought up and embellished just before the next game. This form of motivation is often used effectively by team managers, such as the one who told his team: "Now it's a right dirty bunch we are playing today, boys, so go out there and retaliate first."

The Realities

There are more important things in rugby than remembering laws or even having a theoretical grasp of the elements of the game. Here are some simple rules to make an impression on the rugby field.

1. Never try to play at anything but the lowest possible level. It is the fact that you are playing which impresses people. They won't be any more impressed if you are playing for the fourth XV rather than the fifth. Many clubs might try to force you to play at a higher level, but stand firm. Apart from anything else, going into a higher team will usually ruin your social life.

2. Never worry about how you play. If you play at the right level, a red haze falls over everyone's eyes about three minutes after the game starts which doesn't clear until after the fourth pint in the bar. Therefore no-one will know what you did on the pitch until you tell them afterwards. (If you are playing in a game with spectators, you are being far too ambitious and should drop down a few teams.)

3. Never be in too much of a hurry to get to your feet after tackling, or to leave a **ruck** or **maul**. It is far safer and less demanding to roll about on the ground than to do something foolish like chase the ball. If you have any doubts about how to do this, watch your props for some advanced techniques.

4. Never be close enough to the play to miss a vital tackle. Everyone remembers the poor soul who let the winger side-step him. They don't remember the other 14 bods trundling along miles behind the play.

5. Never run with the ball. If, by accident, you get the ball, pass it as quickly as possible. Running with the ball is very tiring and can be hazardous to your health. It is far better to let someone else take the blame for losing it to the opposition.

6. If you are a forward, never wear a vest or T-shirt under your jersey, no matter how cold it is. This is enough to get you branded as effeminate by the **front row union** for all time. Backs can, of course, wear vests (they will be regarded as effeminate by the front row union no matter what they do). If you play on the wing, you are probably best to wear thermal underwear, a couple of warm sweaters and an anorak.

7. If you are, say, playing second row, and discover in the first lineout that your opponent is 6'8", 20 stones, with a shaven head and HATE tattooed across the knuckles on both hands, whatever you do, don't show fear. Let him take the ball, then limp off the park with a recurrence of your painful groin strain. (See Injuries & How to Acquire Them.)

Here are a couple of tricks or ruses that can be used to psych out your opponent.

The Difficult Move Manoeuvre

In rugby, as in most other areas of human endeavour, it is more important to appear to know what you are doing than to be able to do it. This isn't at all difficult. Just try a highly sophisticated manoeuvre the first time you get anywhere near the ball.

For forwards this could mean something adventurous like passing the ball or trying to 'sell a dummy' (the act of pretending to pass the ball – normally regarded as an extremely dangerous manoeuvre as it encourages players to late tackle you).

Backs have to try something even more complicated. This could involve performing a double loop while shouting a succession of numbers and code words. Dropping the ball in this manoeuvre will be of little consequence. The mere fact that you tried something difficult will convince your opponent that you know what you are doing and he will spend more time watching you than watching the game.

If your 'difficult move' is done with enough panache, it will also allow him to tell everyone in the bar afterwards that you were pretty good but that he managed to shut you down.

The Positional Play Ploy

It is a good idea to impress upon your team-mates the stress you place on positional play. With your experience you don't go running off blindly after the ball but read the game and position yourself where the ball is going to be.

This is based on a theory evolved by a group of bluffing props which states that if you stand in any part of the field for long enough the game will eventually come to you. The problem with it is that you may well find yourself in the right place at the wrong time and actually have to do something.

Advanced bluffers will often stand just behind their own goal posts, so as to be handy for charging down the conversions when their opponents score.

The Short Lineout Ruse

Forwards, when particularly out of breath, can always take a breather by staying out of a lineout when they have the put-in. If you are not there, your opponent will have to run madly out of the line (or give away a free-kick) making him twice as breathless.

The Dirty Jersey Move

If the ground is muddy it is important that you get your jersey covered in grime as early as possible. For most bluffers this involves running to the worst part of the pitch and rolling about while everyone is up the other end of the field. A dirty jersey has two advantages:

1. It makes it look as if you have been tackling and were tackled.

2. If it is muddy enough, the referee will have great difficulty giving a penalty against you for being offside.

THE POSITIONS

Before you can advance in rugby bluffing (in either a playing or a non-playing capacity) you must choose a position for yourself. This will depend largely on your size and shape. For example, any player who is more than 6'3" and 18 stone with a broken nose need not try to convince anyone that he is a full-back. He could have the defensive qualities of Gavin Hastings or the attacking skills of Serge Blanco but he will still end up playing second row.

Non-players should choose a position that is either the most gruelling or the most romantic available to their body type. Players should choose the position that is least damaging to their health, or least likely to show their lack of ability.

Here is a list of the positions, complete with the most common topics of conversation and details of the advantages and disadvantages of each. Also included are a few famous players. Knowing their names will establish you as a good player far more than any ability on the pitch.

The Pick a Position Method

The first thing to get right is whether you are a **forward** or a **back**. In soccer the forwards are the fast, skilful ones who score the points and the backs are the big, vicious ones who try to injure forwards. In rugby, just to confuse, the situation is completely reversed. That is, except for New Zealand, where everyone is fast, skilful, big and vicious.

It is usually decided by weight. If you are three stone

overweight for your height you'll be a forward; two and a half stone overweight and you'll be a back. Once you have decided where your allegiance lies you must insult the other group of players at any opportunity.

Forget about team spirit. For example, the one group of people a rugby forward hates more than the team down the road is the backs in his own team. And the only people he hates more than them are the players in the teams above and below him in his own club.

The Forwards or The Pack

Forwards like to be called 'the pack' as they feel it gives them a menacing, ravening quality. This can be slightly spoiled if you see them halfway through a game, unless you expect wolves to be overweight and balding with sweaty, red faces and chronic asthma.

Props (No 1 or 3)

Officially there are two props in every team, but as it is the one position where you are not allowed to retire before you are 50, this can lead to a surfeit in many sides. When players are in short supply, teams have been known to play with eight or nine props filling every position from wing to scrum-half.

There are two types of prop: the **tight head** and the **loose head**. There is a rumour that this has to do with which side of the scrummage they stand on but in fact it has more to do with a physiological problem that afflicts their necks.

Their job is basically quite simple. They stand on either side of the hooker in the scrum and hold him up. To listen to them, however, you would soon gain the impression that propping, as a science, is only slightly less complicated than landing Concorde. They also stand near the front of the lineout and assault anyone in the opposing team foolish enough to jump.

Ideal appearance: Props can be virtually any height from 4'8" to 6'2", though small props are very popular. Small props will tell you that a good small prop will always 'get under' a big prop. This means that big props often fall on little props and break their ribs.

They can be any age from 28 to 60, although 40 plus is common. Nobody knows what props do before they are 28 but they certainly don't prop.

The common denominator is that without fail they will be anything from five to 14 stone overweight. This is called 'giving the scrum solidity' and is based on the theory that the other side will tire themselves out having to push that much fat about.

Because of their weight problems they are excused running, pushing and jumping. If they get involved in a ruck or maul it is usually by accident.

Typical conversations: Props talk a language of their own and will only ever be seen talking to other props and hookers. As the only part of the game they see is the scrum, they seem to think this the only thing that happens in a match. A prop can come off the field after your team lost 98–0 totally convinced that you won because he 'lifted' his man three times and 'took one against the head' (q.v.).

Advantages: No running or jumping required.

Disadvantages: Playing in the front row hurts a lot.

Names: Fran Cotton, Frik du Preez, Graham Price, Sandy Carmichael, David Sole, Ollie le Roux.

Hooker (No 2)

There is only one hooker in every side and most teams are lucky to get that many. The hooker is the poor soul who is stuck right in the middle of the scrum where he is supposed to 'hook' the ball back to his scrum-half. But if you listen to his props you will quickly discover that his efforts are totally superfluous as they hook the ball for him.

It is one of the great ironies of modern rugby that the hooker is also expected to throw the ball into the lineout. This requires him to interpret lineout codes correctly *and* have the hand and eye coordination to get the ball to the correct player. As the hooker is 'the player most likely to suffer concussion' this is a fine example of the optimism that afflicts most rugby team captains, e.g., "Come on boys. We can still beat them. It only needs five converted tries."

Older bluffers should bemoan the day they stopped wingers throwing the ball into the lineout. Some wingers have never touched the ball since.

The position of hooker is traditionally filled by the person who is too slow or too small or too fat to play anywhere else. It is the one position that should be avoided if at all possible. This is chiefly because you are not allowed to be injured if you are a hooker.

Hookers want to prove that they are tougher than the big men they play alongside. This may well be true but is a very silly thing to try to prove. It results in hookers playing on with injuries that would have second rows being rushed to hospital with the blue light flashing. For instance, a hooker with a broken leg is expected to hop to scrums shouting "It's all right. I'll strike with the other one". Anything less would be considered bad form by the front row union.

Ideal appearance: Hookers should be as short as is humanly possible. There is a tendency for some top class teams to have 6'2", 16 stone hookers. This is fine, for instance, in the Australian front row where the props will be 6'5" and 18 stone. But it doesn't work at club level. Anyone who has seen a 6'2" hooker who has just played a game with two 5' props will realise where the design for the question mark came from.

Typical conversation: As per the prop's conversation, except that they seem to think that they hooked all the balls and took the two 'against the head'.

Advantages: You will always get a game. The most unlikely looking people will be happily accepted as a hooker.

Disadvantages: Your chances of surviving the game are pretty slim. Worse still, you might find you enjoy it. Ex-hookers are expected to come out of retirement up to the age of 75 if called upon.

Names: Peter Wheeler, John Pullin, Daniel Dubroca, Keith Wood.

Second Row (Nos 4 and 5)

Second-row forwards are so called because they push in the second row of the scrum. This is why you should always refer to them as 'locks'.

They are traditionally the 'jumpers' in the lineouts. This is an honorary title with no real meaning.

An interesting feature of second row play is that apart from watching the ball fly over your head in the

19

lineout and under your feet in the scrum, you might not see it again in the game. Second rows don't count the number of tries they scored in a season but the number of times they had the ball in their hands.

This is because they arrive late to every break-down. And not just because they are slow. As locks can't leave the scrum until the back row has gone, it is quite logical not to arrive at the break-down until after the back row (although anything over 35 minutes would be regarded as excessive).

They should, in theory, arrive at the second phase break-down after the front row. In most club games waiting for the front row to arrive is like waiting for grass to grow on the practice pitch. Luckily at this standard of rugby, second-phase possession only happens once every three or four seasons. As the essence of rugby bluffing is arriving at the point of play just after the ball has gone, this is the perfect position.

Ideal appearance: The one thing you need to be as a second-row player is big. It's handy if you are big and fat but being big is often good enough. However the definition of big varies according to the level you are playing at. At international level 6'10" is regarded as barely sufficient. At Old Queens' Fourth XV anything over 5'8" will do.

The other distinguishing feature of second rows is that they tape or bandage their ears. This is to stop the backs of their ears getting split when they pull out of the scrum too quickly. Other posers (like props and flankers), who tape their ears, do so because they like dressing up.

Typical conversations: Most of the after-game talk is taken up with finding out what happened during the game. Most spectators are closer to the play than the average second row and a shortsighted player might not even know what team he was playing against.

Advantages: No need to run or tackle. You are encouraged to drink a lot to keep your body weight up.

Disadvantages: You should really try to push in the scrums, and wave your arms about in the lineouts.

Names: Willie John McBride, Walter Spanghero, Colin Meads, Andy Haden, Bill Beaumont, Wade Dooley.

Number Eight

The number eight is the one who pushes in the middle of the back row and locks the whole pack together. This is why he is called the number eight. It remains the same even if the team number their jerseys in reverse order or in letters of the alphabet.

The number eight also jumps at the back of the lineout. This involves standing waiting for the ball to bounce off the flailing arms of the second rows and fall into his arms – one of the more impressive moves in rugby.

There are several disadvantages to playing in this position. You are supposed to push in the scrum, control the ball coming out of the scrum and even sometimes pick it up and run with it (unless the scrum-half gets hold of it first, of course). The number eight is also part of the back row so is supposed to run around the pitch tackling people. Luckily most number eights ignore such nonsense and stroll around the park at about the same speed as the second rows.

Ideal appearance: To get this key position, you obviously have to have the correct physical attributes. You should be (at least) 6'6" and a wiry 14 stone. Quite why there are so many 5'8" podgy number eights is, therefore, a bit of a mystery.

Typical conversation: The number eight will spend the whole evening after the game trying to work out why none of the back-row moves worked out. In fact it's because back-row forwards are congenitally incapable of remembering codes and carefully crafted moves. Most have difficulty remembering the words for *Swing Low, Sweet Chariot*. But you can never seem to convince a number eight of this.

Advantages: You have a chance of seeing a lot more of the game than the second row.

Disadvantages: If you did everything you were supposed to, you would drop dead with exhaustion. Even when you retire you are supposed to stay thin and wiry.

Names: Brian Lochore, Mervyn Davies, Jan Ellis, Dean Richards, Benoît Dauga.

Flankers

If a rugby side is short of numbers to make up a team, they play without flankers. Perhaps it is significant, therefore, that there are always people queuing up for this position.

The reason is quite simple. Flankers have no responsibilities. They don't jump in the lineouts or push in the scrums. In fact their only real job is to run round the pitch tackling anything that moves. As it is the responsibility of each back to tackle his opposite number, they can even pass the buck for missing any vital tackles. What more could a bluffer want?

There are two systems for positioning flankers in scrums. You can play 'Right and Left' or 'Blind-side and Open'. Always insist that your experience is of the other system to the one your team uses. If given the choice, pick 'blind-side'.

In the old days flankers used to be called 'wing forwards' but this title was dropped because it didn't rhyme with anything.

Ideal appearance: There are two kinds of flanker – the boyishly enthusiastic and the psychopathic. Neither are particularly pleasant company for an evening.

The enthusiasts should be tall, thin and athletic, preferably with blond hair. The psychopaths just need a cold, mad glint in their eyes. The one thing a flanker should do is to put the fear of God in the stand-off who will then usually throw the ball away if a flanker gets within half a pitch's length of him. The boyish enthusiasts fail pathetically at this.

There are a vast number of small flankers who will insist that you don't need to be big and strong to play this position; that it's more important to be fast over the ground and have good technique. Team selection committees always choose a big lumbering forward for this position if they get the chance (i.e., if he's not playing second row). However flankers who need to be lifted on to bar stools are still quite common.

Typical conversations: Telling the number eight to "Shut up about *!***ing back-row moves".

Advantage: No-one will pick a fight with you just in case you are one of the psychopathic ones.

Disadvantages: When centres miss their tackles they start bleating 'Where was the back row then?' The answer is obvious. Late tackling the stand-off.

Names: Piet Grayling, Fergus Slattery, Jean-Pierre Rives, John Taylor, Ian Kirkpatrick, Roger Uttley, Tony Neary, John Jeffrey, Neil Back.

The Backs

Half Backs or Five-Eighths

It depends on whether you are in the Northern or Southern hemisphere as to whether these players are half-backs or five-eighths. The five-eighths title was introduced by the Antipodeans in a futile attempt to persuade everyone they were good at maths. This ruse was seen through when New Zealand television announced that the All Blacks had beaten England 'A lot to three'.

Scrum-half (No 9)

The scrum-half forms that vital link between the pack and the backs. As such he is 'the player most likely to get tackled'. Speed and agility can make a difference of course. If he has enough of these qualities he becomes 'the player most likely to get late tackled'.

He has to put the ball into the scrum in such a way that the first person to touch the ball is the second row in his team. It is achieved by a technique similar to the googly in cricket. He then takes the ball out of the scrum, assuming that it came out where he expected it to (unlikely) and assuming that the number eight hasn't pinched it first (highly unlikely).

As if he didn't have enough problems, he is the person the forwards slap the ball towards in a line-out. To understand what this is like, imagine waiting to catch a lofted ball in cricket while standing in front of a herd of stampeding buffalo. If that sort of thing appeals you have the makings of a scrum-half.

As the only people on the park who know what it feels like to have a rugby ball in their hands, the greedy little rats usually go on to take quick penalties, drop-outs, kicks for touch, argue with the referee and drink most of the jug in the bar after the game.

Typical appearance: It is possible to have a tall scrum-half but unlikely. For anyone big enough to play in the forwards, it is much more fun stomping all over the opposing scrum-half than being stomped on by eight hairy forwards. Usually small, wiry and bruised.

Typical conversations: Scrum-halves talk about rugby all day, everyday. Well, you would have to be enthusiastic to play in that position, wouldn't you?

Advantages: For a player, being the scrum-half means that you are the pivot around which every move is made. For a bluffer, there are no advantages in being a scrum-half.

Disadvantages: For a full list read our '9,000 Reasons For Not Playing Scrum-Half' published in six volumes.

Names: Gareth Edwards, Sid Going, Nick Farr-Jones, Jacques Fouroux.

Stand-off (No 10)

The stand-off or fly-half or 'the $**!**! who kicks the ball every time he gets it in his hands' is the next link in the chain between the forwards and backs. As such he is shunned by both. As a group, stand-offs are not friendly to anyone either – getting a reputation for being stand-offish.

He is the first player to receive the ball from the scrum-half at scrums or lineouts (in the event that the forwards actually win the ball, of course). He is also the one player with a special dispensation from ever attempting to pass the ball.

Anyone with difficulty passing the ball could therefore try this position although there are some obvious disadvantages. These disadvantages usually take the shape of two psychopathic flankers. It appears that stand-offs are also the only people on the pitch excused from tackling. Advanced bluffing stand-offs actually need to be quite nimble on their feet to get out the way of any opponents running towards them with the ball in their hands.

Appearance: Selectors try to choose a tall thin stand-off. This is simply to make the little, dumpy scrum-half he is standing next to, look silly.

Typical conversations: Stand-offs spend every Saturday evening in the season explaining to irate centres why they kicked every time they got the ball.

Advantages: You don't need to pass or tackle.

Disadvantages: Psychopathic flankers. Some flankers have been known to late tackle stand-offs who have been retired ten years.

Names: Barry John, Naas Botha, Michael Lynagh, Phil Bennett, Grant Fox, Gregor Townsend.

Three-Quarters

It is cruelly suggested that backs are called three-quarters because they spend three-quarters of their time running about without ever touching the ball. This is untrue. In a normal club game they will spend all the time running about without touching the ball.

Centres (Nos 12 and 13)

There are two centre positions on the pitch: 'inside and outside' centre or 'left and right' centre. When playing for the first time find out what system is used, then claim your previous club used the other one. It's not much of an excuse but it's better than nothing.

The **Inside Centre** runs about the centre of the pitch shouting at the stand-off, 'If you'd passed there I'd have been in', every time he kicks.

The **Outside Centre** has similar duties except that he has to shout at the inside centre.

An inside centre may specialise in the 'crash ball', where he runs into his opponent head first. This is by far the most successful ploy that can be used by any bluffer's side, because:

a) it drastically cuts down the chance of the backs dropping the ball
b) the forwards don't have far to run, and
c) you can play one of the six spare props as a centre.

The main disadvantage with the crash ball is that, if you are playing against a bluffing centre, he will probably jump out of your way and you may have to run quite a distance before anyone tackles you.

Ideal appearance: Centres should be tall, dark, handsome and fit-looking. That is perhaps why the position seems to appeal to small, squat people with skin complaints and beer bellies.

Typical conversations: A centre's conversation is the rugby equivalent of the fisherman's 'One that Got Away'. Titles of books written by centres include *The 100 Best Tries I Could Have Scored* and *101 Things to Do While Waiting for a Pass*.

Advantages: Pick the right stand-off and you never need to worry about getting tackled.

Disadvantage: If you ever do get a pass, you are so surprised you don't know what to do with the ball.

Names: Mike Gibson, John Dawes, Will Carling, André Boniface, Philippe Sella, Scott Gibb, Jeremy Guscott.

Wingers (Nos 11 and 14)

In a perfect world wingers would be thin, lithe and exceptionally fast. In most club rugby, wingers are the people that are left over when everyone else has been given a position.

In the top flight clubs it may well be worthwhile having someone fast on the wing. But in grass-roots rugby the likelihood of the ball getting to the winger without being dropped or kicked is so remote, no team would think of putting a good player there.

In the lower reaches of rugby being a winger is exactly the same as being a spectator, except you get to wear the club jersey and you can't be offensive to the referee.

Typical conversations: No-one really knows what wingers talk about. It is presumed that they are pretty philosophical. Standing about with nothing to do all day is inclined to make you think deeply.

Advantages: None.

Disadvantages: On some pitches your zimmer frame can get caught in the mud.

Names: David Campese, Rory Underwood, Gerald Davies, David Duckham, Brian Williams, Jonah Lomu.

Full-Back (No 15)

The full-back is often a rather pathetic, lonely soul. It is his responsibility to be the last person to miss the tackle before the other side score a try. If the game is going well for the team, everyone forgets he is there. If it is going badly, he takes the blame for not being able to tackle all seven players running towards him.

It is vital that he should be 'good under a high ball'.

To most full-backs this means saying their prayers while waiting for it to come down. It is also important to shout 'Mark!' in an imperious voice as the high ball slips through their arms and bounces off their knees into the arms of the opposing centre. As if that wasn't enough, they often want the responsibility of missing the place kicks as well.

The full-back is no better off when playing for a good team. He may not have to do so much defending but the team will expect him to come into the attack. The average player would need to lie down and dab his forehead with lavender water if he had to run from the full-back position to where the three-quarters stand. If he then had to start sprinting towards the line it would just take all the pleasure out of the game.

Ideal appearance: As few players actually know they have a full-back, little attention is paid to what they look like. To flankers, the opposing full-back waiting for a high ball to land will often look a bit like a baby deer caught in the headlights of a speeding car.

Typical conversations: These are usually with the team manager or selection committee member and start 'I was wondering if next week I could get a game on the wing?'

Advantages: If you don't like your team-mates very much you don't really have to mix with them.

Disadvantages: As the player furthest back on the pitch you don't have anyone to pass to.

Names: JPR Williams, Serge Blanco, Andy Irvine, Gavin Hastings.

THE OTHERS

There are a number of other key people involved in every game of rugby. It is not suggested that you should volunteer for any of these posts. In fact, you would be better avoiding them like the plague. But you should know where they all fit into the pattern of things and how to treat them.

Referees

Rugby referees are nothing like the meek, inoffensive lot you get in soccer or tennis. Rugby referees are a bad-tempered, touchy bunch who would give a penalty against you for parting your hair on the wrong side (Law 2,763, paragraph 3a: 'No player shall enter a maul with hair combed in any direction other than that which the referee deems correct').

There is no point in arguing with them. The only time a referee will change his mind is when he starts giving you a severe talking to, thinks better of it and sends you off. Half a word of dissent means an immediate penalty and the other half means a penalty ten metres further on. In some games, the referee has been known to give so many penalties like this that the last one has been taken from the middle of the main road running along the end of the pitch.

Under the circumstances you should never challenge a referee. Instead, restrict yourself to saying "Is this ten metres, Sir?" in a tone that suggests you are saying 'I think your mother was a baboon'.

Luckily the laws most referees are really hot on are 'dissent to the referee' and 'off-side', so details like assault with a deadly weapon and kidnapping of the opponents' scrum-half are often glossed over.

Touch Judge

This is a vital and onerous task traditionally carried out at club level by a man walking his dog past the pitch and a little old lady who only came in to ask directions to the Bingo hall.

At international level the touch judge can inform the referee if he sees any foul play. In some places (especially Wales) the touch judge seems to be able go on to the pitch and punch any player on the opposing side that he thinks is involved in foul play.

Selection Committee

People often say about rugby 'I wouldn't like to play rugby. I wouldn't like to get hurt.' This shows a basic lack of understanding of the game. No rugby player likes to get hurt. You don't go on to the pitch to get hurt. You go on to the pitch to hurt other people. In fact, the only true symptoms of clinical masochism shown by anyone to do with rugby are those displayed by the selection committee members.

They spend hours deliberating every week as to how to get that subtle blend of as many players as possible playing:

a) out of position

b) for a team they don't want to play for, and

c) in close contact with people they don't like.

Having got this 'ideal' mixture they have to stand about from Thursday evening to Saturday morning, watching all their hard work unravelling.

It is also traditional for them to have flaming rows with the players they have dropped. They then have to go back to them on Saturday morning to ask them to play because the player chosen in their place has 'gone shopping'.

To round off a perfect day, they take the blame for the fact that every team gets beaten.

Spongeman/Team manager

The titles spongeman and team manager are interchangeable. If you are playing in a team where they are not, drop a few teams.

It is the vital task of all spongemen to make the players think they are not as badly injured as they really are. Every week a spongeman, somewhere, sponges down a broken collar bone with cold water saying, 'Just try and tackle with the other shoulder'. Or, 'Honestly everyone has eight pints of blood and you've only lost about five.'

Captain

The naïve may think it a great honour to be asked to be captain. Put all such thoughts from your head. Captains, like all good heroes, are supposed to lead by example. This means that team-mates will expect you to catch the ball cleanly, run and tackle – all the things that any sensible player tries hardest to avoid.

If asked to take on the captaincy, demur modestly and suggest the person you like least in the team should be given the honour. That'll teach him.

Pack leader

If it is important to avoid being the captain, it is doubly important to avoid being the pack leader. The captain simply has to moan at the players for five minutes at half-time, while he is standing still. The pack leader is supposed to moan at the forwards throughout the whole game while he is running around.

Pack leaders are unable to shout anything good to their side. You can be leading 72–nil and the pack leader will still be bellowing, 'They're just walking all over you', or 'Haven't woken up yet, have you?'

They are obsessed with meaningless phrases like 'Let's get there first'. This is shouted when the ball has been kicked into touch and the pack leader wants his players to run to where the lineout will take place.

As everyone knows that lineouts were invented purely to allow forwards to catch their breath, this sort of action is both pointless and irresponsible.

THE KEY ELEMENTS

Rugby is made up of several distinct elements. Fortunately it is unnecessary to learn about all of them. Once you have chosen a position for yourself, you need only study the elements that apply to you as a **forward** or a **back**.

Despite the fact that backs spend most of the game watching the forwards in scrums and lineouts they have only the vaguest idea of what is going on in them. Conversely, there are a number of forwards who have never realised there is such a creature as a back, thinking that any winger they meet on the pitch is a prop with anorexia.

The Warm-up

You often hear terrifying stories of warm-ups where players bang their heads against the door and punch themselves in the face to get 'psyched up' for the game. The reality is somewhat different. The warm-up involves players hanging round the bar, drinking, while the team manager telephones everyone he knows to try and get hold of a prop and two wingers.

The Kick-off

The game starts with the forwards lining up opposite each other looking fierce. As the kicker runs towards the ball, his pack trundle forwards for all the world as if they expected the ball to be kicked somewhere near them. This is a clever ruse. The kicker instead kicks the ball to the opposing full-back who returns it an extra 22 metres or passes to his three-quarter line who run the length of the pitch and score a try. Forwards need do no more than stand about looking surprised.

When one side scores (this is usually the opposing side and it happens about forty times a game) play is restarted with a drop-out from the centre line. This is obviously more unpredictable and it has been known for the ball to drop where the forwards expect it, by pure chance.

The 22 Metre Drop-out

It is supposedly impossible to score an own goal in rugby (although many players would disagree when they look at the team sheet – see Selection Committee). If the opposing team kick or carry the ball over the line and then fail to touch down for a try, a drop-out at the 22 metre line is awarded.

Normally the term '22 metre line' is never mentioned (except by the French who like that sort of thing) and by Mini-rugby players. If anyone mentions a drop-out on the 22 look at them in amazement. On the other hand, if you're trying to avoid being picked for the Veterans and someone mentions '25 yard line' simply ask "What's a yard?". That usually works.

Open Play

Open play is the time when you watch naïve players running about like headless chickens. With the right referee this is only a minor part of the game, some-times taking up less than three per cent of playing time.

The highlight of this phase of play is the break-down. (Remember that the definition of the break-down is where the ball carrier is stopped, not what stand-offs suffer when they find that the other side has good flankers.)

When the ball carrier is stopped, either a ruck or a maul is often formed. The only one most players need worry about is the ruck. For a maul to form, the ball carrier must:

a) not drop the ball when tackled, and

b) not fall down when tackled.

Mauls are therefore something you practise on training nights, when you don't want to get muddy.

Forwards anywhere within walking distance of a ruck are almost obligated to get involved. The only exceptions are back-row players and, of course, front-row players, who regard themselves as too good to get involved in such unseemly tussles. When you consider that the second rows are usually too far behind the play to get involved, you can see that rucks can be quite exclusive affairs.

What the players do instead, is 'fringe' – a move where they wander aimlessly around the ruck waiting for the referee to give a penalty against them for being off-side. However, smart forwards spurn all this fringing nonsense and plough straight into rucks. This is an excellent opportunity to have a rest and catch your breath. You don't have to go running after the ball like the idiots who fringe.

The Lineout

A lineout happens after a back kicks the ball out of the field of play in the mistaken belief that this will stop the flanker tackling him. Or it can happen when the back doesn't kick the ball out of the park and the flanker kicks him into touch while he is still holding on to the ball.

The two sets of forwards then line up beside each other, staring menacingly at their opponents (this is important). A player on the side that has to put the ball into the lineout shouts out a code involving 14 numbers and three random words. This is the lineout code and is loosely based on the kinds of German codes that computers were invented to crack during the Second World War.

This does not take into account that the average lineout jumper wouldn't grasp the fact the ball was being thrown to him if the lineout call was 'The ball is going to be thrown to you, George. OK?'

The real purpose of lineout calls is so that hookers and jumpers can blame each other for losing the ball. The hooker then throws the ball to one of his own players and looks hurt when the referee gives a free kick for 'not-straight'.

At the more advanced levels, lineouts become a fascinating tactical battle. They are virtually a game within a game, working on a very similar set of rules to volleyball, but without a net.

The major difference is that volleyball players are supposed to slap the ball to the ground in their opponents' court. In contrast, rugby forwards try to knock the ball to the ground on their own side just far enough from their own scrum half to ensure that he has no chance of catching it.

In the lower echelons of the sport, play is often simplified, with players confining themselves to elbowing their opponents in the ribs and pulling jerseys during lineouts. They are often so occupied in this pastime that possession of the ball is only decided when it bounces off someone's head and goes to the other side.

Some of the terms for the lineout need to be understood. The players to whom the ball is supposedly being thrown are known as **jumpers**. Many beginners mistakenly believe that this comes from the verb 'to jump' – to propel oneself into or through the air by the power of one's legs. In fact it comes from the old English verb 'to jumper' – to stand waving one arm in the air while holding on to your opponent's jersey.

Lifting in the lineout – the hazardous habit of props grabbing a second row by the shorts and hoisting him into the air – has somewhat lost favour in bluffing rugby. It usually meant that there was a greater chance of the ball bouncing off the 'jumper's' head and dropping into the arms of the opposition, so it was rather counterproductive. Given the excessive weight of most third-team second rows, this is not recommended.

The Scrum

Scrums were invented as the only way for forwards to keep warm on cold days. This is why they spend so much of their time telling backs just what hell it is in there – in case they should want to come in too.

To be an expert on scrums you must learn some technical terms.

Against the head – This is when the ball is put in a scrum by one team and comes out in the possession of the other. It is normally caused by the hooker kicking the ball forward instead of hooking it backwards. Well, hookers aren't very bright. Why do you think they became hookers in the first place? It is also the sign for bluffing props on the other side to immediately start claiming that they hooked it.

Back-row move – This is where the open-side flanker and number eight both try to pick the ball out of the scrum at the same time and clash heads. At the same moment the blind-side flanker runs off in the opposite direction, turns round looking puzzled and says "I thought with that call we went blind-side".

Three-Quarter Moves

Pass – When one player drops the ball in the process of trying to give it to another player. Forwards can (and usually do) ignore this facet of play. Passing is usually attempted because there are two psychopathic flankers bearing down on the player in question. As a tactic it is virtually useless. Psychopathic flankers will tackle you anyway, whether you have the ball or not.

Reverse pass – When a player throws the ball behind him in the optimistic belief that one of his team-mates is waiting to receive it. He then turns round to discover that the team-mate in question is arguing with a spectator on the touch line or is standing on the other side of the pitch looking confused.

Spin pass – When a player throws the ball a long distance, spinning the ball so that it drops at the feet of an opposing player, miles from anyone who could possibly tackle him. This often results in a try.

Scissors – Where two players (usually backs) run across each other's paths before they drop the ball.

Loop – What happens when, by some quirk of fate, a player gets the ball into the hands of his team-mate without him knocking on or dropping the ball. Flushed with success he then runs to the other side of his team-mate in the mistaken belief that lightning can strike the same place twice. This manoeuvre is only carried out in training sessions, largely because in a real game if anyone is good enough to pass the ball, he is sure to get late tackled by some vicious-looking flanker and won't be able to run anywhere for at least ten minutes.

Tackle – When a player with the ball chances to run into an opponent. To a non-player this may seem an unlikely event. However, there is some mental aberration in the personality of all forwards that causes them to insist on running into someone on their way to the line. Some big forwards have been known to come back after crossing their opponents' try line without scoring, looking for someone to run into. A tackle can be carried out by all the players on the park although this is not obvious from watching most games.

Drift defence – When the backs drift all over the park hoping their opponents will run into them by accident. Backs playing for a new club or team should ask "Do we use drift defence?" if for no other reason than the amusement of seeing the blank looks on everyone's faces.

Tactical Kicking

Tactical kicking is what you do when you see a psychopathic flanker bearing down on you. It is also often used by backs who realise that, by kicking, they can avoid running with the ball.

The material thing to remember about kicking is that if anyone on your side kicks the ball within 20 metres of you, it's the sign to start moaning about the fact that he should have passed to you as you were "wide open". This ploy seldom fails since:

a) he is probably concussed from the late tackle, and

b) he probably didn't know you were on the field, far less that you weren't 'wide open'.

Quick penalties – This is when you take a penalty by tapping it with your foot and running at the opposition with the ball in your hand. It is supposed to catch the other team by surprise. It is only carried out when you realise your kicker couldn't kick the ball into the Grand Canyon five feet from the edge. As the other team always realise this before you do, it never seems to surprise anyone except the person to whom the ball is passed.

Since the only real advantage from winning a penalty is a chance to catch your breath, this sort of nonsense should be discouraged.

Type of Kick

There is a whole sub-culture in the game involved with kicking. The wise will avoid it. Nothing shows your lack of ability quite like trying to kick the ball.

The shape of the ball was carefully chosen by the founding fathers of rugby to be precisely the shape to be the most difficult to kick in any given direction. And just in case anyone did manage to get the knack, they invented several different methods of kicking, to make it more difficult.

Place kick – Where the kicker takes a while to achieve the feat of making an oval ball balance on one end and proceeds to kick it – in the opposite direction from that intended. It can be used for kick-offs and for missing penalty kicks at goal and conversions. Don't believe the kicks that international kickers pull off. It is all done by mirrors.

Punt – The classic 'Quick, here come the flankers' kick. It looks so easy that even forwards will try it occasionally. Don't – unless it looks likely that you are going to be tackled, in which case anything is worth a try. It is this kick that is used in penalties when a team is kicking for touch. This is where your best kicker boots the ball up the pitch as far as he can, if possible straight to the opposing full-back. The full-back then returns the ball, using the same kick, and the ball will go backwards and forwards in this way until someone kicks it out of play by accident.

Drop kick – A highly skilled manoeuvre where the ball is dropped and kicked the moment it touches the ground. As backs have more experience at dropping the ball than anyone else it is usually left to them. This is used for drop-out kicks, most kick-offs and quite often when the stand-off gets the ball 15 metres in front of the opponents' line at which point he will insist on kicking the ball ten metres to the left of the posts.

Fly-hack – The equivalent of soccer's 'big boot up the park'. It is the kick most loved by forwards, because it allows them to kick any opponent lying on the ground while pretending to be aiming at the ball.

You can pick out the soccer player who has converted to rugby because he insists on kicking the ball every time he gets it in his hands. He is traditionally picked as stand-off.

The Point of the Game

According to the law-books, drinking ten pints of beer and singing rude songs are not the real purpose of the game. The aim is to score more points than your opponents. Props should note that, contrary to popular belief, no points are given for taking a ball against the head and flankers should realise that the scoring of points is regarded as more important than having your opponents' stand-off carried from the pitch on a stretcher.

The points are scored thus:

Try – 5 points. A team scores a try when the ball is touched down over their opponents' try line. There are no points for getting the ball over the line and dropping it, which is a pity as this happens eight or nine times a game. There is a story that it was called a try because in the old days no points were given, but the scoring team had the opportunity to 'try' to score by converting it into a goal.

The real meaning is rather more mundane. It is called a try because you have to try not to kiss and cuddle each other like soccer players when it happens. After you see some of the forwards you would have to kiss and cuddle, this is not as hard as it sounds.

Conversion – 2 points. Once a try is scored you have the opportunity to convert it by kicking the ball between the posts and over the cross-bar from any-where on a line from where the ball was grounded. This is possible from everywhere on the pitch except, for some reason, directly in front of the posts.

Drop goal – 3 points. At any time during open play any player can score by drop-kicking the ball between the posts. This would in theory give three points but is so unlikely as to be not worth remembering. Until relatively recently a drop goal was always awarded more points than a try – a rule brought in by the one man who could drop-kick accurately.

Penalty – 3 points. Whenever the referee gets bored he is allowed to award a penalty (usually for off-side) to the team nearest their opponents' goal line. In theory this should allow the attacking team to score three points by kicking the ball between the posts. In practice it is done to humiliate the kickers.

THE LAWS

As many have always suspected, there are no rules in rugby, only laws. This is to add gravity to proceedings. It gives the impression that getting off-side is really a criminal offence and you were lucky to get away with just a penalty. It could have been six months' hard labour.

Keep in mind that there are more laws applying in rugby than the Soviet Union had under Stalin. This provides enough to ensure that the referee can find an infringement roughly every 35 seconds in order to keep up with the play.

There are so many laws, the referee can blow the whistle and then think of an infringement, such as 'I'm giving a penalty for running with the ball within 20 metres of your opponents' try line' or 'I'm awarding a free-kick for not putting the ball in straight at the kick-off'.

Because of the difficulties involved in trying to keep track, it is simplest to apply the bluffer's **Suitable Law Interpretations** method which involves learning two or three simple infringements that can be applied to each facet of the game on a strict rota system. This is the same system many referees use.

Lineout Interpretations

There are absolutely no laws regarding lineouts. It is true that the use of hatchets, machetes or flick knives is frowned upon but may be ignored if the referee wants the play to flow. This is because, by the end of a lineout, the referee will have caught his breath and doesn't need to stop the play.

If a penalty is given at a lineout it is usually done on a mathematical formula. For instance, one side may have committed seven infringements compared with five on the other side.

There are only four infringements at lineouts which are worth remembering. When the hooker throws the ball to his own man it is 'not straight'. Otherwise it's 'jumping across the line', 'closing the gap' or 'barging'. Technically they are roughly the same infringement but referees have invented these names for them, so you might as well use them too.

A free-kick can be given for standing too close to your opponent in the lineout. How wide 'the gap' is changes regularly, so if you stand behind the player in front of you, you can always blame somebody else.

It would be a real gaffe to suggest that a penalty was given for elbowing your opponent in the face. This is accepted as part of every lineout and is seldom commented upon.

There are laws governing how far back you can stretch the line but these have been changed so often that it is unlikely anyone remembers what they are. The only referees likely to give penalties for an offence here are master bluffers – a very dangerous and frustrating breed.

Scrum Interpretations

Wheeling – The ruling bodies have introduced a number of laws to ensure that scrums continue much longer than they did before. Now every time the scrum wheels (goes round and round) you start again.

This means that referees can keep scrums going for anything up to half an hour. Some scrums wheel so much and so quickly that the forwards get dizzy and have to sit down for a minute.

Collapsing or *Dropping the scrum* – It is difficult for sane people to understand, but there are props who take delight in collapsing scrums and having 15 people pile on top of them. To add to the props' fun, the law makers have introduced a rule which states that every time this happens you start the scrum again, allowing them to collapse it again.

It is, of course, an offence to do this deliberately. This is enforced by giving penalties against each front row in turn, unless the scrum is near to your goal posts, when the penalty is given to the other side.

Not straight or *Feeding* – The scrum half is required to put the ball into the scrum along a line directly between the two front rows. Tell-tale signs of a *not straight put-in* are:

a) the ball being put in along a straight line between the second row and the back row, or

b) the first player to touch the ball is the number eight.

Open-play Interpretations

Knock on or *forward pass* – With that indefinable sense of logic that pervades all the laws of rugby, the only direction in which you are allowed to pass the ball is the opposite direction from the way you want to go.

Thus any time the ball is passed forward or goes forwards from a player's arms (for instance when you are crunched from behind by a 20 stone second row) you have a scrum (or sometimes a penalty if the referee is in a bad mood). This seldom happens more than 3,000 times a game.

Killing the ball – A law, based on the unlikely notion that players want to jump on the ball and get kicked to pieces to prevent the other side getting possession. The truth is people fall on the ball from sheer exhaustion after having had to run to the break-down. The related law, *not staying on your feet,* is unfortunately very popular with refs on TV and is therefore used a lot. Every second penalty given in open play will be for this. Luckily it doesn't seem to apply to the drinking session afterwards.

Late tackling – Another area of play that referees are keen on. Flankers, hurtling themselves full stretch at the stand-off at 100 miles an hour, are supposed to stop dead in mid-air and drop gently to the ground if they see him kick the ball away.

Therefore flankers prefer to tackle the stand-off a full ten minutes late, at a time when the referee is safely at the other end of the pitch. A penalty is given for this infringement, either where the offence took place or 'where the ball alights'. This can lead to some interesting situations where penalties are taken from the middle of the main road or someone's back garden. Note that kicked rugby balls never land. Like bus passengers they always 'alight'.

Off-side – Off-side is a God-send for referees as it is possible to find players off-side at any moment in the game and for several hours after it. You can be off-side at the kick-off, at scrums, lineouts, in open play, in the bath after the game and in the bar.

There is absolutely no point learning about off-side. Top internationals are supposed to know all the off-side laws yet they find themselves off-side (usually in front of their own posts) 10 or 12 times every game. This is because off-side laws are tremendously complicated. For instance, if you are in front of the ball when it is kicked, you may not tackle the opposing player unless his name is Fred and he drinks lager.

Here are a few practical examples of off-side infringements you can quote.

Coming in on the wrong side – This is an area of confusion. Players are often aggrieved when penalised for this, thinking that it has something to do with the direction from which one enters a ruck or maul. This is a fallacy. The 'side' talked about here is actually the team (or side) for which you play. For instance, to a Devon referee any Somerset player is 'coming in (to the game) on the wrong side'.

Not retiring – Supposedly to do with being in front of the ball when it is kicked but actually given against ageing props for stopping younger players getting into the team.

Fringing or *Not being bound on* – A penalty given for milling about in rucks and mauls getting in everyone's way. Quite right too.

One source of reassurance to all backs is that these fringing laws prevent them coming anywhere near lineouts and scrums. Most backs need no more encouragement and will often stand as far as half a mile away.

Accidental off-side – This is a clever ruse by referees to make it appear that all other kinds of off-side are done on purpose. This happens when a player with the ball runs into his own player. Don't laugh. It can happen quite easily, honestly.

Penalties and Free Kicks

There is a complicated formula for whether a penalty or a free kick is given for an infringement, worked out on phases of the moon and direction of the wind. However it is important to recognise when a free kick has been awarded. The referee bends his arm instead of giving a full Nazi salute.

While you can't charge a penalty you can charge a free kick, from the moment the kicker 'presents the ball' (or as it's termed in English 'makes a move to kick'). Some of the wilier players will, at this moment, distract the referee's attention. As soon as he turns his head the flankers violently assault the kicker claiming that he 'presented the ball' while the referee had his back turned. Hours of innocent fun here.

Archaic Laws and How to Use Them

Because of the vast number of law changes over the years, one way to validate your credentials is to know at least some archaic laws and appear to forget that these laws have changed. Apart from anything else the referee may forget that the laws have changed and play by the old rules. This happens normally in the course of most games.

It is perhaps overplaying things a bit to quote things like '*All matches are drawn after five days or after three days if no goal has been kicked*' (Law 32 from the first standardised set of RFU rules evolved in 1871). But here are two to try.

Forced into touch – In the good old days if a player was kicked into touch holding on to the ball, the put-in at the lineout went to his side. Not much consolation for the player in question but worth the hooker shouting "Forced into touch" in a confident tone and trying to take the throw-in.

Calling for a mark – It is only in the last 20 years or so that you were restricted to calling for a 'mark' or fair catch inside your own 22 metre line. It is therefore worth shouting for a mark in the unlikely event that you catch the ball cleanly anywhere in the park.

The conditions for taking a mark are continually being eased until now it is possible to make a mark while skidding along the ground on the seat of your pants. If the opposing full-back calls for a mark and the referee blows his whistle, it is worth tackling him anyway, pointing out that he only had two feet on the ground when he did it. It will certainly discourage him from catching the ball again.

INJURIES AND HOW TO ACQUIRE THEM

It is always handy to have an injury to fall back on, and the best place to receive the injury is playing for your present club. Injuries from previous clubs are regarded with extreme suspicion. However, if you are of a naturally nervous disposition there are a number of other methods of acquiring acceptable injuries.

Training sessions

Training sessions are the ideal place to get injured. For a start, everyone will be impressed that you have actually attended a training session. It is more than any of your team-mates will do.

Veterans' matches

Veteran teams are supposedly restricted to players over 35 but this excuse can be used by players of all ages above 25. In fact, a good 25-year-old could easily find himself playing for the Colts on a Saturday and the Veterans on a Sunday without comment.

Naturally you don't really want to play Veterans' Rugby. It would be putting yourself amongst the masters of rugby bluffing. But you could make a quick guest appearance. For example, in some veterans' games up to half the team have been known to sustain serious injuries in the act of putting on liniment before the game.

Pub teams

Pub teams form an excellent source of long-term injury. This is largely because both teams are so well lubricated when the game starts that after it they have no recollection of who was playing, far less who got injured. It is, therefore, possible to get injured in a pub match without getting out of your bed on a Sunday morning.

What Injury to Acquire

There are certain traditions as to what sort of injury you should have. Forwards usually have back and shoulder injuries, backs have leg injuries. With a little imagination you could think up some really interesting ones for yourself. You could have "an impact fracture of the wallet" or "badly stretched bounds of credulity".

Your chosen injury can be a recurrence of a previous injury, of course. This happens regularly because playing members usually pay substantially less membership fees than non-players. This means that some clubs have around 25 per cent of playing members permanently injured, including some in their late eighties. They will usually appear at training, early in the season, and hobble off after ten minutes bemoaning the fact that they have tried to come back too early from an injury they sustained in 1952.

Inexperienced players are sometimes worried that if they don't play one week they might not get a game the next. Bluffers know better. After a grudge match there are so many real injuries the team captain will welcome you back with open arms.

INTERNATIONAL RUGBY

Each rugby nation has a distinctive style so it is possible to appear knowledgeable just by injecting one or two key-words when that nation is under discussion. These words can be applied to each team and to individual players in those teams.

If players don't fit in with the key-words of the team they will never make it at top level, no matter how good they are.

England
English teams are *solid* and *methodical*. England is famous for gathering together some of the fastest, most skilful backs in the world and then never passing the ball to them. This is because teams like Scotland and Ireland live off the mistakes made by backs. If you have big, strong forwards who can get you the ball, why risk giving it to the puny little backs who might lose it? They also might score tries but that is not considered important.

The Celtic nations have developed a little practical joke where they take turns to beat England in the last game of the season to stop them winning a Grand Slam. The English do not find this very funny

Scotland
Scottish teams are *spirited* and *fiery*. They also scavenge for the ball. This means their forwards aren't big enough to get the ball themselves so they wait until the other side drops it and then pick it up.

This is a tactic they have used with such success that they now get confused when they get possession and don't know what to do with it.

For some reason Scottish players can have strong New Zealand or even English accents. This is accepted by the Scots as long as they beat the English.

Wales

Welsh teams are *gritty* and *determined*. Discussions about Welsh rugby usually end in nostalgic reminiscence about the Glory Years.

The secret weapon of Welsh rugby was that it was played by miners and people who did manual jobs and were fit. When pitted against the English teams, they naturally annihilated them. Then the English Rugby Union teams discovered it was possible to get fit by training and similar underhand tricks. And English Rugby League teams discovered that they could keep the Welsh international team permanently under strength by offering key players vast amounts of money to play the 'other code'. Now these Rugby League players are coming back – much fitter, faster, stronger and more skilful than they went away. It perhaps wasn't as good an idea as it first seemed.

Ireland

Irish teams are *plucky* and *brave*. This means that they nearly always get beaten but, luckily, they don't seem to worry about it.

Rugby is virtually the only sport that draws its players from the North and South of the country for an all-Ireland team. Compared with this achievement, it hardly matters whether they win or not.

It was an Irish international who uttered the most famous quote in rugby: 'Nothing takes the edge off your game like training.' For that alone every Irish team should have the support of all true enthusiasts.

As the team that is always expected to lose, the Irish take great delight in upsetting everyone by occasionally winning.

France

French teams are *brilliant* but *erratic*. What this means is that if they are winning, they are very friendly. When they start to lose, they suddenly want to punch someone. Ironically, they seem to want to punch one of their own players as often as they want to punch the opposition.

French teams also have to have 'the sun on their backs' to win. This is based on the fond notion that France will lose simply because it rained for ten minutes an hour before the game started.

Italy

Italian teams are *emotional* and *physical* – not a good mixture to find in your rivals. After years of taking turns at coming last in the Five Nations, it was probably the Celtic Nations who thought it was a good idea to become the Six Nations and allow Italy to be the regular Wooden Spooners. This theory has been rather dented by the fact that Italy have already managed to defeat or nearly defeat most of their opponents. You just can't trust some people.

New Zealand

New Zealand teams are *clinical* and *hard*. They play percentage rugby, which means that the opposing side's score should be a percentage of their score – usually quite a small percentage.

Always beware of any country that is only famous

for two things. New Zealand is famous for rugby and sheep and the sheep aren't anything out of the ordinary. Because of this New Zealand can't quite get the game of rugby into perspective. The All Blacks losing is a good reason for the government to fall, especially if it ever happened against a Northern hemisphere side.

A while ago they discovered they could win every time by doing sly things like having forwards who were fast and fit. And, by always passing the ball when they were tackled, not allowing the opposition any time to catch their breath.

The All Blacks are famous for their *haka*, a war dance performed at the start of each game. This instils fear and dread in their opponents who know that if they had to perform a *haka* before the game, they would be so tired they would have to lie down for ten minutes.

Australia

Australian teams are *rugged* and *strong*. Australia got interested in rugby simply because it gave them a chance to beat England. Any game where they have this opportunity seems worth taking up, no matter how unlikely (e.g., cricket). It makes it even more fun to beat the English at a game they invented.

Strangely enough this motivational force can also be seen in Ireland, Scotland, Wales and France and most of the 'emerging nations'. It does not apply to New Zealand and South Africa who just like to beat anyone – usually to a pulp.

These days Australia's main aim is to beat New Zealand. Now that they can do that, there isn't much left to do.

South Africa

South African teams are *hard* and *fast*. In practice this means playing dirty, but no-one can catch them to punch them.

The real problem with South African rugby is that the country is too hot to have a proper rugby season. This means that anyone foolish enough to play in South Africa has to get used to playing on pitches that make concrete seem soft and springy.

Compared to the pain of falling on the ground, the normal knocks and bumps that rugby players endure seem trivial. This creates a breed of rugby players without a properly developed fear of pain.

They demonstrated how vital it is to be experienced at international level by swanning back after years of isolation and beating everyone.

Fiji/Samoa/Tonga

Recent years have seen the emergence of the South Sea teams – huge men who love to run about passing the ball. If anyone ever tells them that real rugby is not like that, they will cause a lot of problems.

Fijians are famous because they can always beat the senior nations in seven-a-side tournaments (which have to do with running about passing the ball). But get 15 of them together on the pitch and they keep knocking into each other.

The Samoans upset everyone when they discovered it was much more fun tackling the other side than running with the ball.

Romania/Argentina

As well as the standard rugby nations there are the odd pockets of rugby throughout the world. With the strong British tradition in Argentina there is almost an excuse, but no-one can begin to guess why people play rugby in Romania. It is also impossible to say why these teams go on tour and get slaughtered and then proceed to beat the best in their own country.

Canada/America
The Canadians and Americans put out teams of huge, strong, fast men (like American footballers with the padding still on) who look as if they should beat everyone. If they ever learn how to play the game this could well happen.

Japan
Only the Japanese can come to a World Cup delighted because they have at last found two second rows over 6' tall. As if they didn't have enough problems, every time they get a penalty they don't kick at goal because this would be dishonourable. Instead they take a quick penalty and get their 6' second rows to run straight at their 7' opponents. To everyone's delight, they often nearly beat the big sides that are supposed to slaughter them. For that alone it is worth buying one of their cars.

The British Lions
The British Lions team does the impossible by bringing together the four Home nations to create a British team. Selectors have a completely free hand. They can pick the best players from every nation so long as England have no more than five players, Ireland have no less than two, and every nation is represented.

GLOSSARY

Pitch – A piece of open ground where, it is said, grass grows during the summer. Traditionally used for exercising dogs.

Player – Someone who can't get out of the club quickly enough when he hears the fourth XV are short of a winger.

Replacement – Another name for a spectator.

Spectator – Mythical creature that was claimed to prowl the touch lines of rugby matches shouting suggestions at the referee.

Open play – Part of the game when everyone else runs around.

Foul play – What the other side does. If your side does it, it is called 'using your initiative'.

Forwards – Large players who don't run around.

Backs – Marginally thinner players.

Dummy – The person persuaded to replace an injured hooker. Also the act of pretending to pass the ball while still retaining it – one of the few times you will be tackled by a flanker without winning a penalty for being tackled late.

Pass – What you do as quickly as possible if you get given the ball by accident. Also see Knock on.

Possession – When your team has the ball. Can happen three or four times a game.

Maul – Something the All Blacks and Springboks do. Does not apply in bluffing rugby.

Ruck – Informal, impromptu get-together for forwards and a few close friends.

Mark – The free kick you get if you can catch a ball kicked several hundred feet in the air within your own 22 metre line and call 'Mark' while the opposition is pounding towards you intent on changing your shape. You deserve it.

Off-side – A natural break in the play called by the referee every 35 seconds to let everyone get their breath back.

Blind-side – The art of being on the side of the pitch where nothing is happening.

Break-down – What happens when the stand-off gets tackled.

Drop-out – What the full back becomes at 11.30 on a Saturday morning when his wife decides he is needed for shopping.

Knock on – See Pass.

Side-step – A move, perfected by bluffers, to get out of the way of an opponent running towards them with the ball.

Front-row union – A secret organisation that any sensible player will avoid joining.

Other code – Euphemism for the type of rugby you don't play.

THE AUTHOR

Alexander Rae developed the main theories for bluffing rugby when he discovered, early in his playing career, that he was useless at the game. Never to be one to let such details stand in the way of his enjoyment he quickly evolved a style of play that removed the need to run, jump, tackle or touch the ball.

Putting these theories into practice he has played in every position in the field except full back and scrum-half (well he isn't that stupid) although he prefers to play flanker in which position he is said to be a little reminiscent of John Jeffrey. (No, not that John Jeffrey – another one.)

He would still be playing today except for a bad back injury which will probably clear up later in the season. He is Scottish but moved to Somerset some years ago in the mistaken belief that the Scottish were going to continue winning Grand Slams.

For the rest of the week he is a freelance writer, which is a far more dangerous and painful occupation.

THE BLUFFER'S GUIDES®

The million-copy best-selling series that contains facts, jargon and inside information – all you need to know to hold your own among experts.

AVAILABLE TITLES:

Accountancy
Astrology & Fortune
  Telling
Archaeology
The Classics
Chess
Computers
Consultancy
Cricket
Doctoring
Economics
The Flight Deck
Football
Golf
The Internet
Jazz
Law
Management
Marketing
Men
Music

Opera
Personal Finance
Philosophy
Public Speaking
The Quantum
  Universe
The Rock Business
Rugby
Science
Secretaries
Seduction
Sex
Skiing
Small Business
Stocks & Shares
Tax
Teaching
University
Whisky
Wine
Women

www.bluffers.com